Productivity Secrets

More time. More money. More freedom.

Sean Combs

Table of Contents

Set a Game-Plan!

One factor that all successful people have in common is effective time-management. You may prefer to call it structure, setting yourself to the task, or a game-plan. Whichever word or term works for you is fine. As long as you take it seriously, and put it into practice, you are creating one of the basic principles of productivity.

It might be a good idea to think about this, and why this factor is so essential to success. Perhaps you can begin by thinking of the opposite-- ways which do not work. Even if you have one very small task to complete, if you do not manage your time appropriately it may get done too late, or not at all. You may be working on a deadline, or have a task which does not have a specific time to be completed. If you do not have a game-plan for getting it done, the results will not be satisfying. While procrastination and wasting time impede productivity, lack of effective time-management can be as destructive.

Increasing your productivity and getting things done means having a good game-plan. First, you need to know exactly what must be done. Second, even if you do not have a specific deadline, you must also decide when it must be done. The third step is putting yourself to the task of doing it.

You want to accomplish your goals, whether they are short-term or long-term. You also want to be proud of and satisfied with the results. When you are not content to simply "go with the flow," and instead take your game-plan seriously every step of the way, you are nearly guaranteed of success, pride, and satisfaction.

Structure and time-management may come easy for you, if they have been a regular part of your life. If you are not used to these concepts, now is the time to implement them into your everyday life. Whether you are setting up a business of your own, working for someone else, or whether your work is taking care of your family, you will reap many benefits from setting up a good game-plan.

If you have ever felt that there are not enough hours in a day to do everything you need to do, this will be a very positive step for you. You will be pleasantly surprised with how much you can accomplish. With a game-plan, you may find yourself getting more done each day than you usually accomplish in a week. Not only will you be more productive, but achieving

each goal will come much easier. You will soon
appreciate this all-important factor in your success.

Reducing Distractions

There are few things which block productivity as fast and as surely as distractions. When you cannot concentrate and focus properly, you cannot get things done. Even if you do accomplish something, it can feel stressful and frustrating. Whether you are on the job or at school, reducing the distractions which influence your ability to be productive will help you to get more done.

There are two key points that you should keep in mind when you are planning to reduce the distractions in your environment. The first point is what works for you and what works for someone else may be entirely different. The second point is unless you have examined your habits, you may not be one hundred percent certain about the habits that are the most effective for you. The good news is it does not require much time or effort to consider how your habits are affecting your productivity, and begin to adjust them accordingly.

If you are like most people these days, multi-tasking has become a part of your everyday life and your everyday vocabulary. There may be a number of things that you need to do in one day, and you may be doing them simultaneously. If you overdo with multi-tasking, there can be two consequences. You might not get everything done; or you might spread yourself too thin and not have satisfactory results.

The same can be said about distractions. Attempting to do a job-- and to do it correctly and well-- will not net satisfactory results if distractions are allowed to get in the way. Working while listening to music, watching television, or chatting on the phone are not limited to teens. Many adults do these things in their home offices, and even in an office that is occupied by other people. Perhaps they help your concentration-- but they can just as easily ruin your concentration, and distract you from what you are doing. Becoming more productive takes a little analyzing of your habits. You can turn off some or all of these distractions, and see if you are better able to focus on the task at hand. You may find that you can get the job done better, faster, and more effectively, without any distractions at all. On the other hand, you may find that one of these factors actually does aid in your concentration and focus.

While finding whatever works for you is easy if you work on your own, it can be a little more complicated if you work with others. You may find that coworkers who constantly use their phones, visit, or play their radios near your workspace distract you from focusing on your job. If you approach them politely, this may be all it takes to reduce the distractions so you can concentrate on your job.

What Should You do First?

If you think about back when you were in school, you may remember teachers telling you that the best way to approach homework and other projects was to do the hardest task first. They may have also advised you to tackle the homework subject you disliked the most first, before moving on. This same approach can greatly enhance your productivity today.

When you are preparing to begin a fresh day at work, try to begin putting this approach into action. Instead of beginning with a task you enjoy, or one which comes easily to you, start with one you dislike, or one which you feel will be quite difficult. At the end of the day, you may be pleasantly surprised with how much you have accomplished. You will also feel that the day has gone much smoother.

One reason for this is at the start of your workday you will have more energy. When you devote this energy to the hardest or most disliked tasks, you will not feel as drained or frustrated in doing them. A second reason is if you begin with tasks you enjoy, you often find yourself looking ahead to the ones you dislike in a very negative manner. Instead of enjoying the easier tasks while you are doing them, you are dreading the ones ahead. When you do the hardest ones first, you will not only have more energy left for the rest of the day, you will also appreciate the other tasks more when you get to them.

This approach will increase your productivity. When you do not look at your work day as a long, uphill battle, you will get more accomplished. Getting the tasks you dislike out of the way first, early in the day, will generate better results with all of your tasks. Not only will you get more done, you will be much more satisfied with the outcome of each and every task.

While it is only human nature to want to do what you like first, having the harder things on the horizon can slow you down and drain your energy. If you want to be more productive, and achieve the very best results in everything you do, take the advice from your schoolteachers and tackle the hardest jobs first. Your productivity will increase, and you will end each day with a refreshing feeling of accomplishment.

Exercise Self-Discipline

Self-discipline is an essential factor for productivity and success. Without it, one becomes lazy, unmotivated, and dependent upon others. Lack of self-discipline also makes for a difficult-to-deal-with employee, boss, or coworker.

Exercising self-discipline means, in an old-fashioned term, setting yourself to a task. You need to know what must be done, when it must be done-- and do it. Good self-discipline includes a basic schedule, or framework, of what needs to be accomplished within a specific period of time. You do not allow yourself to become sidetracked, or to procrastinate.

However, being too rigid with self-discipline does not increase productivity. It can even lessen it. If you do not allow yourself any breaks throughout the workday, or any room for error at all, the expectations you are placing on yourself are too rigid. Instead of getting more done, or doing more in a shorter period of time, it can cause you to become frustrated with your tasks and your job.

If you learned self-discipline early in life, you probably do not have any difficulty with it now. On the other hand, if your schooling years and family life were too rigid, or if little was expected of you, this is a good time to develop the habit. You may have managed to slide through your early years without a good sense of self-discipline, but it will be a stumbling block to your career.

A good way to start cultivating self-discipline is to acknowledge what you are responsible for. You can begin by holding yourself accountable for getting the job done correctly and on time. If this is a relatively new concept for you, you also need to acknowledge that errors do occur, and be able to fix them without undue frustration.

Exercising self-discipline also includes not allowing yourself to be sidetracked by time-wasting distractions and activities. While you may need and deserve a little break during your workday, it cannot throw you off-course from getting the job done. When you have developed the habit of self-discipline, completing tasks will be easier. They will be done well, and on time. It will increase your productivity, and help you to move that much closer to success.

YOU CAN DO THE IMPOSSIBLE

If you have ever had so many different tasks to complete, or tasks that appeared to be beyond your capabilities, you know what it is like to feel that it is impossible. When these kinds of tasks are within your range of responsibility, there are some positive ways in which you can approach them. You may find that you really can do the impossible.

Sometimes you may see tasks as impossible because you are overwhelmed by how much you need to do within a short period of time. Even if each is quite simple, they can add up to a mountain of work which you cannot reasonably expect to finish. This can happen when you take on more than you can handle, or when unexpected "surprises" come up without adequate preparation.

A positive approach to the former situation is to be reasonable about what you can do in the beginning. Whether taking on too much is due to financial necessity, trying to look good for your boss or outdo a coworker, or not thinking it through when you take on each task, assessing your capabilities beforehand can eliminate this problem. A positive approach to the latter situation is to learn how to prioritize. If an unexpected assignment or project comes up while you are tending to your other duties, you should decide which tasks need to be completed immediately, and which ones can wait until later. In many instances, requesting more time to get everything done is a good idea.

Sometimes you may have a project that really is beyond your capabilities. In these cases, the best approach is to acknowledge your limitations. Depending upon the circumstances, you can ask for help or state that you are unable to do it.

Good time-management and a clear acknowledgement of your abilities are the keys to doing the impossible. Instead of being overwhelmed by work, or stressing yourself out over something that you are simply incapable of doing, you will be increasing your energy and your self-esteem. While no one can do everything, and no one can do everything equally well, you will be proceeding to the very best of your ability. This, in turn, will reduce the feeling of being overwhelmed, and will help you to be much more productive.

Increasing Motivation

We have all heard people state that they were "not motivated" as an excuse for not getting things done. In most cases, this is a polite way of saying that they are lazy. In the real world, where productivity and success are essential, motivation is a key element. If it does not come naturally to you, you can examine ways to increase your own motivation, and put it into action every day.

The more motivated you are, the more you will get done. One way you can try to increase your motivation is to both enjoy and appreciate your accomplishments. Instead of holding off until you have attained your goal, begin by enjoying and appreciating every task you complete along the way. While you should not want to waste time or become sidetracked, giving yourself a figurative pat on the back for tasks completed well and correctly can be a great way to increase your motivation. You will want to do more; and you will want to continue to excel.

When you do this, it will also help to increase your stamina. Rather than feeling overwhelmed by one main goal on the horizon, which can leave you tired and stressed, it can make you feel more energetic and better prepared for the next task.

It is easy for a person to lose his sense of motivation when he feels that he is not accomplishing anything. This can result in him not feeling very good about what he does, and even doing less. Fortunately, it is not difficult to reverse this pattern and come out on top. When you get into the habit of feeling glad about every task you complete, and have pride in each and every accomplishment, it will increase your motivation to do even more, and to do better each time.

As motivation and energy are connected, you will also see that you have much more energy for all of the tasks in front of you. No matter how large your ultimate goal happens to be, or how much time and work you need to put into it to accomplish that particular goal, you will be pleasantly surprised at how much more smoothly it all progresses. As both your motivation and your energy increase, you will get more and more done. You will see how great productivity can be each day.

Don't let Setbacks get You Down!

One of the biggest roadblocks to productivity is an approach that many people take to setbacks. If you see a setback as a failure, it cannot only limit your productivity but it can go as far as to prevent you from doing anything at all. This is true in any line of work, schooling, or any other area in life. When you see a setback as a failure, it can stop you from proceeding forward. You may accomplish less-- or you may accomplish nothing at all.

Setbacks occur in all areas of life. Regardless of what type of job you have, you probably experience them either occasionally or on a regular basis. Setbacks can occur from making mistakes, from not being adequately prepared for what you need to do, or from unexpected problems which are not anyone's fault. The way you experience and view a setback determines how it will affect you and your productivity.

However a setback occurs, there is one outlook that can prevent it from becoming a roadblock, and actually increase your productivity. Whether the setback was due to an error on your part, or whether it was no one's fault, refusing to see it as a failure is the first step in getting you back on track.

The second step is to see the setback as an opportunity to do better the next time. If you have made an error in your work, the best approach is to try to correct the error and move on. While it is essential that you not try to cover up a mistake, you cannot afford to allow a mistake to cause you to stop. If you fail to correct it and move ahead, you may find yourself dwelling on it. You may beat yourself up about the mistake, or even obsess about it. These behaviors are never useful. Not only will they prevent you from getting things done, they will also cause you to feel bad about yourself. At its worst, it can lead you to feel incompetent. This is not the way to get things done.

Viewing each setback as a learning experience is a much better approach. You can tell yourself that you are capable of doing better, and capable of doing more. As long as you look at setbacks this way, instead of as failures, they will not prevent you from moving forward. Correct the mistake and learn from it, and move ahead. When you have developed this pattern, and make it a regular part of your work life, setbacks will not stand in the way of being productive.

Be Goal-Oriented

"If you don't know where you're going, you might not get there." New York Yankees player and manager Yogi Berra was right on-target when he made that statement. It is an excellent thought to keep in mind for your work life.

You may be surprised at how many people do not know what they are aiming for in their work life. On the other hand, you might be one of those people yourself. If so, now is the time to become goal-oriented. When you know where you are going, that is one of the biggest steps toward ensuring that you do get there.

When you are preparing to go to work in the morning, what is the very first thought to cross your mind on the subject of your goal? If you are like many people, you do not think about it in terms of a goal at all. Instead, you may be thinking about how much work you will have to do, or how nice the paycheck will be at the end of the week. If you shift your thoughts to a goal, you will be much more productive.

Depending upon the nature of your job, goals can take a variety of different forms. You may have something to produce on your own, or you may be a part of a team. You may have a very positive sense of self-discipline, or work very well as a team player. Whichever sums up your place in your work life, being goal-oriented will increase your productivity.

Being goal-oriented does not need to mean focusing solely on one large accomplishment. If you begin looking at it as a number of small goals, each one that you attain will provide two benefits. Each one will make you more motivated to continue, as well as getting you that much closer to the large accomplishment.

Nothing can be accomplished overnight. Anything that is truly worthwhile takes time, effort, and work. When you set your sights on both the large goal in the distance, and each one which you need to accomplish in order to get there, you will soon see how much more productive you will be every step of the way. Simply going with the flow and not placing your emphasis on your goals will slow you down. You will not accomplish much if you do not focus on accomplishing. When you know where you are going, it is the surest way of knowing that you will get there.

Take Care of Yourself!

If you are like most people, you have probably had the experience of working all night to get something done. You may have gone without sleep, skipped meals, and other important factors in self-care, for the purpose of finishing a task or meeting a deadline. While it is sometimes necessary to do this, neglecting self-care on a regular or frequent basis will backfire. Your health may suffer while you are not accomplishing nearly as much as you had hoped.

Taking care of yourself will not only keep you in good health, it will also keep you productive. The person who goes without sleep on a regular basis, or relies on junk food instead of eating nutritious meals, will not be physically or mentally up to par. While you may believe that you are giving one hundred percent to your job, these unhealthy habits result in having less to give.

On the other hand, if you get enough sleep on a regular basis, and make a point of having a healthy diet, you will have more to give to your work. When you are in top-notch condition, you will focus better, be more alert, and not become fatigued as easily. You will do better, and you will do more.

If your workday has consisted of drinking many cups of coffee or other artificial energy-boosters, it is time to examine your self-care habits. If you find that you have not been getting enough sleep, and have been relying on these products to keep you functioning, or if you find that good nutrition has been replaced by junk food and snacks, it is time to assess what these habits are doing to your overall health. It is also time to think about the effects that it may be having on your job.

Although nearly everyone is occasionally in the position of skipping a meal or working late into the night, if these have become habits for you it is not likely that they are helping you to become more productive. In fact, they are probably slowing you down.

Even if you have a fast-paced job with many responsibilities and deadlines, neglecting proper self-care is counterproductive. When you begin developing the habit of getting enough sleep and a proper diet, you will be doing more than taking care of yourself. You will get more done, and be more satisfied with the results.

Why Being Organized is Essential

If you think about it, being organized is one of the most essential factors in being productive. You do not need to be extremely rigid in order to be organized, but you do need to be conscious of and conscientious about everything that goes into your workday. Getting things done means being organized with your time, the supplies and equipment you use, and your expectations.

You can think of someone who is disorganized, and how it affects his work. He may rush willy-nilly into and through the workday, miss appointments, be unsure of what he should accomplish, and be careless with the supplies or equipment he works with during the day. This is a person who does not get things done, because being disorganized prevents him from being productive.

You will get much more accomplished in a shorter period of time if you are well organized. You can begin by making a basic schedule of what you need to do and when it needs to be done. You can make sure that you know in advance where all of your supplies are located, so you will not waste time looking for something when you need to use it.

Being organized with both time and material items is not difficult at all. However, if you have not yet cultivated this habit, it might require a bit of practice before it begins to feel completely natural for you. Preparing an outline of your workday will help you to be where you need to be, and to get things done on time. Keeping all of your supplies neat and organized will help you to avoid wasting time and becoming frustrated over not being able to readily find items when you need them.

When your goal is to increase your productivity-- to get things done-- being organized is an essential factor. If you are one of the many people who have not yet developed this positive habit, the results may astound you. You will soon see that you are accomplishing much more, doing a better job, and ending up with results that are more satisfying. Becoming better organized in every aspect of your work life will greatly enhance your productivity.

When You Need to Delegate

There are two different types of delegating which are both negative. Both can inhibit productivity, rather than increase it. If you recognize either of these factors in your work life, you can begin changing them for better results.

The first negative form of delegating involves the person who wants to do everything by himself. While this may sound positive at first, it actually is not positive at all. The person who insists on taking on more work than he can reasonably do, or work he is not fully capable of performing on his own, not only makes him less productive but also affects the productivity of everyone who is counting on him to do the job. Whether he is afraid to ask for help, or whether he is simply boastful, it can slow everyone else down as well as himself.

The second negative form of delegating involves the person who shirks his own responsibilities. He may ask others to do tasks that he really should be doing himself. Not only is he not carrying his own weight, he is taking up other people's valuable time.

Positive delegating is sensible. When you acknowledge that you cannot do everything, and that you cannot do everything equally well, you are boosting your own productivity in addition to the productivity of those around you.

When you have a very large or very tough assignment or project, asking others for assistance will help in getting the job done, and getting it done quicker. Instead of looking at delegating as an admission of weakness or incompetence, you are acknowledging the scope of your own role and your own capabilities. This, in turn, will give others the opportunity to pitch in and help to get the job done.

Delegating for the sake of doing less than you can do, or less than you should reasonably be expected to do, is always negative. However, when you are up against more work than you can reasonably do on your own, or work which you are not capable of completing on your own, delegating is the sensible solution. When a job needs to be done, and on time, and well, teamwork will give the best results.

Avoiding Burnout

There is very little that can cause a decrease in productivity as easily as burnout. While you may be tempted to believe that putting every waking moment into working on your job is a good way to get things done, there is an additional factor that you may not have considered. When you figuratively take your work home with you, you can increase your risk of burnout and get much less accomplished in the long run.

This form of taking your job home with you does not involve doing some essential work during your free time. It involves keeping your work on your mind during your free hours. When you are at home, or somewhere else other than in your workplace, you can easily burn yourself out by keeping it as your main focus.

During your off-hours, you may put a lot of time into thinking about your job. You may worry about whether you will get something done on time, or the overall quality of your work. This can lead you to become overly stressed, anxious, and overwhelmed. You may become more fatigued by your work when you are thinking about it and worrying about it than when you are actually doing your job.

If you do not actually have work to complete after your normal workday, you can avoid burnout by leaving your job at your workplace when you go home. Instead of stressing yourself out over whatever you need to accomplish the next day, or how much progress you are making with something you are working on, try learning how to leave those thoughts and concerns at your place of business.

When you have free time, develop some positive habits. Learning how to relax, to participate in healthy recreation, and giving both your time and focus to your friends and family will all reduce your risk of burnout. When you have begun to develop these habits, it will not take long for you to see the results. You will start each new workday feeling physically, emotionally, and mentally refreshed. You will have more to give to your job when you are refreshed. You will be more motivated, more energetic, and more productive.

Supplies are a Factor

You may have heard the old saying that a good workman always takes care of his tools. This is equally relevant, whether you work in an office, on a jobsite, or from home. Keeping all of your supplies in excellent working order and easily accessible will make you more productive.

No matter what kinds of supplies you use during your average workday, neglect can slow you down. You cannot do a job effectively if your supplies are broken, damaged, or worn out from use. If you try to use supplies that are not in good condition, the quality of your work can suffer. It can take you much longer to get things done, and they will not be done as well as they would with supplies that are in top-notch condition.

Think of it this way: if you are trying to work on a computer that is not up to par, or using a hand tool that is bent or otherwise damaged, or a piece of office equipment which stalls while you are operating it, your productivity can come to a complete standstill. You may become frustrated or angry, and possibly not get the job done at all.

When all of your supplies, tools, and equipment are kept in ideal condition, they are in better shape to do the job properly. Your work will not be slowed down, and you will not risk errors from faulty equipment. Good supplies in good condition mean getting things done and having the best results.

No matter how much of a hurry you are in to complete a task and end a work day, taking a few minutes to be sure everything is in good shape will save you time and eliminate unnecessary frustration. You can also make a point of replacing damaged supplies or equipment as soon as possible. You can take this positive new habit even further by making sure all of your supplies and equipment are put away where they belong when you are finished using them.

These new habits will benefit you, as well as everyone else who uses the same supplies and equipment. When everything is checked for good condition and put away, they will all be in good condition and easily accessible the next time you or someone else needs them. It will make your workday proceed that much smoother, and you will be more productive.

A Positive Frame-of-mind

Nothing has the power to boost your productivity as surely and easily as a positive frame of mind. While you may not have the time or inclination to repeat affirmations to yourself throughout the workday, it is essential to acknowledge that your mindset influences and affects your productivity.

If you have problems in your personal life, the more able you are to keep them out of your workday the better you will perform. Even if something is especially troublesome, you should try your best to keep your personal problems separate from your work life. If there is something that you need help with, getting help during your free time can prevent it from interfering with your work.

On the other hand, if there is something negative about your work life, it should be addressed and dealt with as soon as possible. Feeling overwhelmed, anxious, stressed, or burdened will only slow you down.

The more you are able to remain positive and upbeat, the more you will accomplish. Even if you are facing a task that is especially large or difficult, a positive frame of mind can help you to accomplish more than you thought you could.

Nothing can be done all at once. Sometimes it takes many small steps to get something done. Sometimes errors and setbacks occur. However, when you keep in mind that each step is getting you closer to your goal, you are on the right track. When you tell yourself that each small accomplishment is an accomplished goal in itself, you are giving yourself the encouragement and the motivation you need for success.

Having a positive frame of mind does not come naturally to everyone. If you are one of the many people who have never put much thought into it, today is the ideal time to start. A positive frame of mind will allow you to feel more confident about yourself, and more confident about your abilities. Even if self-confidence is a relatively new experience for you, you will be reaping the rewards in no time at all. You will soon see how much a positive frame of mind affects how much you get done, and how pleased you are with the results. You will be more productive, and more satisfied with the outcome.

Resisting Negativity

Negativity is a huge block to productivity. It also ensures that anything that does get done is neither satisfying nor appreciated. Whether the negativity you need to resist is your own or someone else's, the quicker that it is dealt with the sooner you will be back on track.

Negativity can come in many forms, and they are all counterproductive. Negativity can come in the form of belittlement. You may be unsure of your ability to do the job, or to do it well. If you believe that failure is on the horizon, this is the surest way of making it happen. You can resist the negativity of belittlement by reminding yourself of your competence. You may need to practice doing this on a regular basis. When you do not allow a negative light to overshadow your abilities, it will prevent you from coming to a standstill.

Negativity can also come in the form of complaining. Whether you are complaining about your job or about something else in your life, this kind of negativity can affect your work. Complaining wears you down, and ruins your ability to focus properly. When you resist the urge to complain every time you feel the desire to do so, you will be taking steps to keep negativity out of your work life. Instead of becoming tired and grouchy from complaining, your energy level will be at its best.

Worry is another form of negativity. It can slow you down, and cause you to be less productive. Although it may sound difficult, a good approach is to remind yourself that worry does not accomplish anything. If the subject is something that you can resolve, doing so as quickly as possible will reduce your worrying. If it cannot be dealt with immediately, try to put the worry out of your mind while you are working. You may even need to tell yourself that worry itself will not solve a problem. This will help you to focus and concentrate better.

If you find that your negativity is extreme, asking for some outside help can be useful. You can learn to be in a better state of mind. This is better for your health in general, and also better for your productivity. The more able you are to resist negativity on a regular basis, the more you will accomplish.

The Tasks for Your Goal

Some people have the habit of looking at their goal as the main thing they need to accomplish. They may even look at it as the only thing they need to accomplish. If this sounds like you, you are missing something very important which can increase your productivity. If you look at each and every task which you need to complete in order to attain your goal as something very important in itself, your progress will be much smoother and you will get more done.

One good way to think about this is in terms of building a house. If you think only about the completed house, you are missing all of the steps along the way. There are many steps necessary for building a house. None can be skipped or done poorly if you want the house to be strong and in excellent condition when it is finished.

The goals you have in your work life are similar. Regardless of what your particular goal consists of, there are a number of steps that need to be done in order to achieve it. For the best possible results, each task along the way requires your time, effort, work, and concentration.

If you have a very important goal ahead of you, you may be tempted to short some of the tasks in between. You may even have the idea that rushing through your tasks will help you to reach the final goal that much sooner. This is never a good approach. When you do not give your very best into each and every task, no matter how small, the final results will not be as satisfactory as you may hope.

Giving your best to each task does not mean making something appear more important than it actually is, wasting time, or forgetting about your ultimate goal. Giving your best means making sure that each task you do receives the time and attention it deserves. It means that you take even the smallest jobs as seriously as you do the larger jobs.

Devoting a proper amount of time and attention to each and every task you do will not slow you down. In fact, it can help you to be better motivated for every task ahead. When you give your best to each one, no matter how small, you are increasing your chances of being completely satisfied with the eventual results when you reach your largest goals.

About Your Coworkers and Employees

There is a trend that is popular in the business world today. Some people believe that competition is the best way to boost productivity. No matter what line of work you are in, it is very likely that this approach will backfire.

First, teamwork is much better than competition. When you use the approach that everyone is working for the common good of the company, more will get done. When the sense of competition is eliminated, each person will want to contribute his very best simply because it is his place to do so. He will not feel that he must outdo his coworkers, which in turn will increase the feeling of teamwork. When everyone is working as a team, and working toward a common goal, productivity will increase.

Second, everyone needs to feel that he is valued. This is as true in the workplace as anywhere else. The best employee, and the employee who gets more done, is the one who believes that his work is appreciated.

Another factor in increasing productivity is to reduce the amount of tension, friction, and conflict in the workplace. When there are employees who make a point of not getting along with others, expecting someone else to do their jobs for them, or simply being difficult to be around on a regular basis, these kinds of problems should be dealt with as quickly as possible. All it takes is one or two people who like to argue, or shirk their responsibilities onto others, to turn any workplace into an uncomfortable place where no one can concentrate on doing their jobs. It is important to eliminate these problems so that everyone in the workplace can get things done.

Productivity is at its best in the workplace where everyone present gets along. This does not mean wasting time with unnecessary chatting and visiting. Simply acknowledging that everyone is there for the same purpose is usually enough.

The workplace should be a place where every employee feels comfortable. It should be a place where everyone knows that his coworkers all have the same goals in mind. When each person knows that he is a valuable part of the company, and a valuable part of the team, each person will feel more confident and will be more productive.

Rewarding Yourself Along the Way

Encouraging yourself by rewarding yourself along the way can be a good thing. Unfortunately, if it is approached the wrong way it can be more trouble than it is worth. If you believe you owe yourself time off, special treats, or something else noteworthy every time you accomplish something, you will soon find yourself accomplishing very little. Instead of seeing it as a reward for a job well done, you may start to feel as if you are entitled to rewards or special favors for completing tasks that are within your scope of responsibility anyway.

This is why granting yourself little "extras" for doing your job is not usually a good idea. It is even more negative if you expect special recognition or rewards from your boss or coworkers for doing what you are supposed to do. Rewarding yourself along the way as if you have made a spectacular accomplishment is not the best way to go about getting the job done.

Instead, applying some self-encouragement should be the only reward you need. When you complete a task on time, or do a project especially well, you can acknowledge it as a small but important success.

When you apply this kind of self-encouragement with a figurative pat on the back, you are rewarding yourself for a job well done. You will also be prepared to move on to the next task or the next step.

This concept works equally well whether you work on your own or in a group. If no one feels compelled to believe that he should gain some kind of special recognition for doing his job, getting the job done will be the priority. In work settings that include a number of people working together as a group, no one will feel more or less important than anyone else. Each person will realize that he is expected to contribute something, without expecting to receive anything unique for doing it.

Encouraging yourself along the way will serve to keep your spirits up and your sense of motivation at its peak. While significant accomplishments may result in some kind of little extra reward, self-encouragement should be the only reward necessary for doing your job.

Resist Overextending Yourself

There are two ways in which you can overextend yourself. You can take on more work than you are reasonably capable of performing; or you can take on work which is beyond your capabilities. Both of these can overtax your energy, cause you to become frustrated, and result in your becoming very discouraged. They also result in becoming less productive.

You may know someone who is a workaholic. He may be finding some aspect of his job to be doing long after he has left the workplace. He may feel that there is always a little something more that he needs to do, many hours after he has left work. This person may feel that no job will get done, or will not get done correctly, unless he himself is doing it.

If you are this person, now is a good time to assess your habits of overextending yourself. While you surely want to be conscientious and complete everything that is your responsibility, overextending yourself will not make you more productive. It may have the exact opposite effect.

Overextending yourself on a regular basis will wear you out, burn you out, and wreak havoc with your health. Allowing yourself to get into this condition can affect your ability to concentrate and focus properly. You may begin making unnecessary errors, or become forgetful. You will not get nearly as much done as you had hoped.

You can resist overextending yourself by being reasonable about both your abilities and your time. Even if you are working on a very important project, you cannot put "24/7" into it and expect it to turn out well. You need to take a reasonable amount of time for rest, eating and exercise, and even some recreation, in order to be in prime condition for doing the job.

Overextending yourself by attempting to do a job that is beyond your capabilities can also backfire. If you are not fully qualified to do it, it will not turn out well. Instead of overextending yourself with something that you know you cannot do, it is better to leave it to someone who really is qualified to complete it correctly.

Becoming discouraged about your job does not need to happen. If you make a point of not overextending yourself, you will be more productive than if you try to take on everything by yourself.

Why You Need to De-stress

Stress has many results, and none of them are positive. The results of stress can stand in the way of getting a job done. Even if a job is finished, the results of stress can minimize your sense of accomplishment and satisfaction. When you de-stress, you will give your best and appreciate the outcome.

As each person is an individual, it can be helpful for you to determine the best ways to de-stress. A coffee break, a brisk walk, or putting your mind on something entirely different for a few minutes, are some ways that may be useful for you. Your own individual personality and needs must be the deciding factors. A method that works for one person does not necessarily work as well for the next person.

If you do not de-stress when it is necessary, you will not get much done. Stress can override your concentration, leaving you focused on everything other than the task at hand. Too much stress, especially if it is prolonged, can make you fatigued and physically ill. In addition to causing headaches and it affecting your general well-being, prolonged stress even has the power to weaken your immune system. At its worst, extreme and prolonged stress can result in medical complications.

When stress has the power to cause all of these problems, it should be easy to see how it can affect your job. This is why de-stressing whenever it is necessary to do so should not be considered a luxury, foolish, or a waste of time. Neglecting the need to de-stress can prevent you from getting anything done.

De-stressing should not be seen as an excuse. Once you have begun to assess the effects of stress on your work life, it should not be difficult to determine when the need to de-stress arises. However, neither you nor your job can afford to use de-stressing as an excuse to be lazy or irresponsible. With only a small amount of practice, noticing when stress is beginning to have an effect on your work will come easy. A little break for whatever specific kind of de-stressing method is most appropriate for you should reduce or relieve your stress. When you are not overwhelmed by stress, it will be easier to focus on what you are doing and get it done.

Setting and Ranking Your Priorities

When you are on the job, virtually everything you do is important. However, setting and ranking your priorities will help to keep everything in its proper perspective. This is a positive way to get things done.

Setting and ranking priorities means acknowledging that some tasks require more time than others, and some tasks require more work than others. If you make the mistake of trying to allot equal amounts of time to every task, it will slow you down and you will not accomplish as much as you should.

While you want to give your best to every task, determining which ones will require more time and effort is a much more productive approach than trying to look at everything equally.

Setting and ranking your priorities also means determining which tasks need to be completed first. You may figure that this is only logical, but it often does not happen that way. Perhaps there is a very large project on the horizon, which will require a significantly larger amount of time and effort than the smaller projects you have at hand. Perhaps there is one that includes an important time frame, or even a deadline. In instances like these, you may have been tempted to do the smaller, easier tasks first. Although it does mean that these easier tasks will be completed, the one that you should have given your attention to first may not.

When you rank your priorities, you can begin by deciding which job or project needs to have your attention before any others. This method will not only ensure that it does get done, but also that you meet it without enough motivation to do it correctly. Similar to what was said earlier in this book about taking on the toughest jobs first, the sooner you begin one with a deadline the more likely you will be to complete it on time.

Setting and ranking your priorities is neither a difficult nor a time-consuming venture. If you begin each workday with a brief outline of everything you need to accomplish, you can then assign top priority to the tasks that must be completed first. Your entire workday will be much smoother, and you will get more done.

Exercising Good Communication Skills

Whether you work on your own or in a busy office, good communication skills should be a standard part of your everyday work life. The better you become at these skills, the more you will get done. In turn, everyone you work with can become more productive.

Some people need to be reminded that good communication skills include knowing the difference between fruitful communication and pointless time wasting. You may have someone in your office that likes to "visit" with coworkers throughout the day, or always seems to be talking on his or her phone. This type of social activity is not appropriate for the workplace. It prevents the job from getting done.

Good communication skills in the workplace can generally be summed up in two categories. There is the type of communication that should be as direct, brief, and to the point as possible. You can say whatever needs to be said, or ask a question, or clarify something, without wasting your own time or the other person's time. The other type of communication is the one that involves giving, receiving, or exchanging information. You may need to fill someone in on an aspect of the job, or request a detailed explanation about a project. In most cases, these are the only forms of communication that enhance the workplace and increase productivity.

Good communication skills also involve being receptive to, and listening to, what the other person is saying. Simply waiting your turn to speak is a negative habit that should have been shed in childhood. If you have not yet developed the habit of good listening skills, it can be helpful to practice this habit during your free time. If you occasionally have lunch or breaks with your coworkers, this can be an excellent time to develop your listening skills.

Practicing good communication skills in the workplace saves time. When questions, answers, and explanations are fully received when they are first spoken, it eliminates the need for repetition. It also gives the other person the message that what he is saying is valuable. When everyone is "on the same track," everyone will get more done.

Strategies are Appropriate Everywhere!

When you hear the word "productivity," the first thing to come to mind is probably your job and the workplace. The good news is that all of these strategies to increase productivity are as appropriate for other "places" in life as well. They are just as useful for students who wish to get more done with their college or high school work, and even housewives who never seem to have enough time to do everything that needs to be done.

There are only twenty-four hours in a day. His is a fact that is equally true for everyone. In the interest of your health and general wellbeing, a number of those hours must be allotted for sleep, some recreation, and other important health-related habits. While this still leaves quite a few hours in the day for getting things done, your time can be misdirected or frittered away if you allow it, or if you are unsure of how to best manage those hours.

The strategies for getting things done are focused on how to best manage your workday hours for the optimum of productivity. When you learn how to not waste time, and to get the most out of each hour and each day, you will get more done. Instead of feeling stressed, overworked, and overburdened, which can all lead to less than satisfactory results, the results you achieve will be real accomplishments.

Developing and practicing these strategies for getting things done will not take much time or effort on your part. Some motivation, and the willingness to begin putting it into practice, is really all that you need. Not only will you see yourself becoming more productive, you can look back on each day as one of your best.

Printed in Great Britain
by Amazon

47287677R00034